WILD
KINGDOM

WILD
KINGDOM

POEMS

Jehanne Dubrow

LOUISIANA STATE UNIVERSITY PRESS
BATON ROUGE

Published by Louisiana State University Press
www.lsupress.org

LSU Press Paperback Original

DESIGNER: Michelle A. Neustrom
TYPEFACE: Requiem Text HTF

Grateful acknowledgment is made to the following journals and venues that originally
published some of these poems: *Arts & Letters*: "*Scholar Sharpening His Quill*"; *Bellingham Review*:
"Swarm"; *Beloit Poetry Journal*: "Memory of a Year with Allusions to the Greeks"; *Birmingham
Poetry Review*: "Minutes"; *Cimarron Review*: "Honor Board Hearing [The student says, the
loneliness of objects bothers me]" and "Honor Board Hearing [The student says, all words
belong to all of us]"; *Copper Nickel*: "Self-Portrait with Cable News, Graffiti, Weather"; *Court
Green*: "Advanced Poetry," "After Crying," "Course Evaluation," and "An Essay on Cruelty";
Diode: "Field Notes on Mobbing" and "Field Notes on the Muted Brilliance of the Female";
Gulf Coast: "Early Mornings in Anger and Thaw"; *Mezzo Cammin*: "In a Tiny College Town"
and "Postcard to the Colonial Town Where I Lived for Eight Years"; *New Limestone Review*:
"Song for a Grackle in the Kroger Parking Lot"; *Ninth Letter*: "Honor Board Hearing [We
say, from the Latin *consentire*]"; *Pleiades*: "Portrait of an Administrator with Strategic Plan and
Office Supplies"; *Poem-A-Day*, Academy of American Poets: "Syllabus for the Dark Ahead";
Poetry: "Fairy Tale with Laryngitis and Resignation Letter"; *River Styx*: "Great Blue Heron";
Ruminate: "Exit Report"; *Shenandoah*: "Anguish" and "Ira Furor Brevis Est"; and *Southern Review*:
"Sun Salutations with Betrayal and Departure."

Cover photo by Lee Avison/Trevillion Images

LIBRARY OF CONGRESS CATALOGING-IN-PUBLICATION DATA

Names: Dubrow, Jehanne, author.
Title: Wild kingdom : poems / Jehanne Dubrow.
Description: Baton Rouge : Louisiana State University Press, [2021]
Identifiers: LCCN 2020022615 (print) ϒ LCCN 2020022616 (ebook) ϒ ISBN
  978-0-8071-7412-8 (paperback) ϒ ISBN 978-0-8071-7502-6 (pdf) ϒ ISBN
  978-0-8071-7503-3 (epub)
Subjects: LCGFT: Poetry.
Classification: LCC PS3604.U276 W55 2021 (print) ϒ LCC PS3604.U276
  (ebook) ϒ DDC 811/.6—dc23
LC record available at https://lccn.loc.gov/2020022615
LC ebook record available at https://lccn.loc.gov/2020022616

Once I witnessed a windstorm so severe two 100-year-old trees were uprooted on the spot. The next day, walking among the wreckage, I found the friable nests of birds, completely intact and unharmed on the ground. That the featherweight survive the massive, that this reversal of fortune takes place among us—that is what haunts me. I don't know what it means.

—MARY RUEFLE

Who but an English professor would threaten to kill a duck a day and hold up a goose as an example?

—RICHARD RUSSO

CONTENTS

a flight of swallows / an exaltation of larks

WILD
KINGDOM

Syllabus for the Dark Ahead

Throughout this course,
we'll study the American
landscape of our yard, coiled line

of the garden hose,
muddy furrows in the grass
awaiting our analysis,

what's called close reading
of the ground. And somewhere
something will yip in pain

perhaps, a paw caught in a wire,
or else the furred and oily
yowl of appetite.

And flickering beyond the fence,
we'll see the slatted lives
of strangers. The light

above a neighbor's porch
will be a test of how we tolerate
the half-illumination

of uncertainty, a glow
that's argument to shadow.
Or if not that, we'll write an essay

on the stutter of the bulb,
the little glimmering that goes
before the absolute of night.

———

a colony of gulls / a siege of herons

Portrait of an Administrator with Strategic Plan and Office Supplies

To sit on her couch was to be silenced
by upholstery, plush muffling of cushions
from which it was difficult to rise.
Arendt writes, *in politics obedience*
and support are the same, and for a time
I was obedient, my reports in ordered bullets:
collaborations, programs, opportunities.
The provost preferred speech contained—
a line of staples in a box. I remember
the fold between one week and the next.
She said to me, *these people are unreasonable.*
She said, *these people are quite reasonable.*
Inside her office everything was cream.
She told me what I heard I hadn't heard,
our last meeting like a memo full of typos
whited out, then shuffled through
the copier machine, language turned to shiny blurs.
Arendt writes, *most people will comply.*
For a time, it was easy to ignore the sharp
wedge of the provost's hair. I should have seen
she resembled more a letter opener on a desk,
how like a knife the piece of metal looks.
I told her what I heard I heard.
I told her that my expertise was words.
Arendt writes, *the holes of oblivion do not exist.*
A gifted bureaucrat, the provost taught me
truth was thin as paper—the little circles
she punched in it remain, and still
I hold this punctured story to the light.

Field Notes on Mobbing

there are birds of prey and birds
          that are preyed upon

the pecking begins before
          the body knows it

what next the wounded throat
          the chest with downy specks

back stippled red
          to pluck bright plumage

is both pleasure and survival
          shrieks resemble laughter

so too in rooks and shrikes
          see diagrams C through E

more research needed
          on the mottled eggs of cruelty

what happens after to the flock
          the brace the cast

the convocation the murder
          the mob the murmuration

Great Blue Heron

The bay is still for now,
like a conference table
undisturbed, opaque surfaces.
What meetings happen here.
I forget the bureaucracy
of seasons, inefficient
changing of the leaves.
I watch from across the water
the yellow light of morning
switching on. In autumn,
the sun sorts through foliage,
a shuffling of papers on a desk,
and the river is a muddied
conversation. Leaf over leaf,
the day does its work
in the vacated offices
where only eelgrass grows,
green spools of tape,
and wild rice like pencils
stuck in the shallows.
If I am migratory, I go
to another cove like this.
These days, I read the shoreline
for the silver gleaming
of ideas, precise and streaking
thought of who I am.

Honor Board Hearing

How much did you consume, we ask, the answer some, as if bellies are balloons impossible to fill, the night unburstable in its own inebriation. Shots are small but take up space. Pints are big but slide inside. We are amazed by these young bodies, floating through the weekend like dirigibles, steered by a crew of strange desires that seem to us as longings from another century, the explorer's thirst for something higher than the sky.

In antique photographs of the disaster, there are pictures taken just before, an airship stretched with possibility, skin taut on metal ribs. But it's after we recall. Flames spread across the frame, ruin that sucks out all the air. We are amazed by these young Hindenburgs, their great capacity for blowing themselves up.

In a Tiny College Town

Our only consolation is to drink
ourselves to laughter, laughing at the slosh
and glug the bottle makes, the world gone pink
as maraschino cherries which we wash
down with soda, a sting of orange peel
around the rim of every glass, a dash
of bitters, a toast to bitterness, what's real:
our laughter in the kitchen and the splash
of ice, sometimes the good crystal and some
the plastic cup, always the slug of rye
or bourbon's caramel, until we're numb—
sleep pretty, you say as a goodbye
and hug me in the porch's amber light.
You leave me laughing in the whiskeyed night.

Scholar Sharpening His Quill

—GERRIT DOU, ca. 1632–1635, oil on oval panel

We've seen this kind of man, this man
hunched in his chair it seems for centuries,
so focused that he forgets the chiaroscuro
of evening coming on, his body forgotten
in its fur-trimmed coat and mottled knot
of silk around his neck, his parchment
face creased with concentration,
seeing something in the darkened well
where the ink is held, *perhaps* or *heretofore,*
the quill in the quavering hand already sharp,
but there he is again with the knife,
slicing the pen tip to an even finer point,
so much of the scholar's work to stroke
his own ideas, to pause in the writing
so that he might consider the keenness
of his implement, feather that was once
a thing of flight, the airy down of it,
now blackened at the slit with thought.

Self-Portrait with Cable News, Graffiti, Weather

When I see the woman on TV, so calm
in her porcelain-white suit, I remember
that I too smiled while a man talked over,
that I bore the persistent tar of his voice.
In those meetings, I watched the veins
in his face like cracks in a disappointed street.
Were it not for his cruelty, I might have said,
I'm sorry for your loss. Who knows.
That year, my husband would overhear me
talking in my sleep, and though he couldn't open
the shut door of dreaming, he told me that I said,
fuck you, into the dark. Quite clearly, *fuck you.*
Night and waking were locked rooms,
the only exit a stuck window,
and the heat was always going or the cold.
Next order of business, a colleague said.
I noted every conversation—on the page,
no one interrupted. Often, remembering that year,
I hold a serving bowl, touch its surface
limned with flowers, this thing
I've dropped or knocked against a shelf,
the way it refuses, decorative, to break.
Now I can say *fuck you* quite clearly to that year,
although there was also the kindness
of friends who brought over cherries—
they knew I loved the sweetness of a stone.
I can say *fuck you.* I will not lose the taste for it.
In that year, I was, truth be told, willing to punch
a fist through glass if it meant escape.
I walked down Greenwood Avenue, past
the house where someone had sprayed FUCK YOU
on the road and someone else had tried

---

to X it out, pale lines on top of lines.
I understood wanting to write one's fury on a place.
I understood even the impulse to erase it,
walking each day across that imperative,
how it disturbed the concrete silence.
Most of us are not the woman on TV
who keeps talking, while the man is shouting
wrong into a mic—she keeps talking while
he stands behind her like a mugger in an alleyway
and who knows what he wants to take.
Most of us are the audience watching the debate—
we comply when the moderator says *no applause,*
no interruptions please. Most of us wait for night
to write FUCK YOU on a clean patch of asphalt.
All of this to say I could have said much more.
I could have written something on the man's sad face.
I think of him. I think of Greenwood Avenue,
its unremarkable houses that I learned to hate—
always moving toward a meeting or coming late from one.
I think of the sound that spray paint makes,
the rattle-shake of the can, the aerosol's soft hiss,
the words emerging slowly on a path, jagged perhaps,
but large enough, remaining legible through rain.

Honor Board Hearing

We say, from the Latin *consentire*. We say, what is your understanding of the word. Did you receive the training, watch the video—when hands may go, when parts may be inserted into parts. If so, you know there must be asked and answered. There must be yes, at every touch a yes. A body sleeping, a body turned to liquid, a body drifting cannot give. The insensible tongue cannot give. It slumps in the chair of the mouth and will not be pushed awake.

———————

When I was done, the student says, she touched me with the tenderness of someone wiping dirt from a child's face. If her underwear was crumpled like a receipt for chips or gum—a thing to toss into the trash—it was only the product of our mutual sloppiness, the way we tripped onto the mattress. It's possible to tumble into sex. We shared the accident of falling. When her shirt was torn, I never heard the tearing. She was not a garment rent in grief. I think about her fingers on my skin, I swear with tenderness. There was no mourning in our contact, no armband wrapped around that night.

———————

The student says, I am a sheet tugged from a bed, rumpled by a careless hand. Who would believe a body laundered of its evidence? Whatever I say becomes a faded stain. When I see him across the room at lunch, he has the sharpness of hospital corners, the kind of credibility that comes from never being scrubbed or bleached. I envy his crisp answers. He seems to have always been this clean, untouched by any history but sleep. There is an ironed freshness in the way he folds himself into a chair, how bright his face, how easily he greets light's inquiries.

———

After Crying

For years, on the college honor board,
I asked about the body and its boundaries—
who owns that place, who enters it.
And then the respondent, as he was called,
would arrange his mouth into a room of grief.
On the TV, a woman is remembering
a hand across her face. She thought
that he might kill her accidentally.
Indelible, she says, *in the hippocampus
is the laughter.* The past is a hallway
that the mind cannot escape. For years,
on the honor board, I spoke with men
(they talked about themselves as boys)
with names like Matt or Brett, who held
their power casually, in the same easy way
they might have carried cans of beer
through a party. A man is weeping
on the screen today. Even now,
he's secure in his confidence like one
of those houses on a sheltered street
where the trees go on for miles.
On the honor board, I saw how we judge
the worth of lamentation—the men,
with their shuttered eyes, their bodies
unbreachable, we place their tears
in bright decanters on a mantlepiece.
We spill the tears of women in the garden
to water the silky roses and the vines.

Field Notes on the Muted Brilliance of the Female

beside the male we say she's drab instead
        of red her crest less like a swoop of flame

emitting from a body made of flame
        in winter less like bloody feathering on snow

than scab the dried complexion of a wound
        we hear his voice the ever what-what-what

and know that he's demanding
        from the world there is no answer

to his appetite the seed he wants the maple sap
        he sips from holes the blossom beaked from elms

beside the male she's modest in her hunger
        but in the nest she's audible at least a note or two

his song the interruption of
        her throat his song repeating louder

what she sang as if the melody were his
        like winterberries stolen from a branch

Piggy

We are perishing
    or publishing, the campus
like that island
    where an airplane
has crashed and we
    are learning how to spear
what we must eat,
    pursuing a pig
through the lush foliage
    of our fears.
We use a pair of spectacles
    to start a fire.
Always someone is fired
    in disgrace.
We send him to live
    at the trees' serrated edge.
All of this continues many semesters,
    which we call the sea,
the way it shoves
    against the rocks
and then retreats.
    Only water now.
Only the throat
    of someone to be cut,
which is to say assessment.
    And soon we forget
to dream of boats
    and who will rescue us,
what marks we'll leave
    disappearing in the sand.

Minutes

Meeting called to order at 4 p.m.
Proposed whom to string with wire
to a wall. Discussed request from
Provost X: a list of volunteers to stand
with hands across their genitalia.
Chair reminded: this is service work,
the music of the flesh when flayed.
New members learned procedure
for abasement, how deep to bend,
the midnight insecurity that is
a colleague's soul. Action items:
the practicality of impalement
on a dying tree, the sort of bird
most qualified to pluck the eyes
from the serving tray of the face.
Professor Whatshisname moved
for a vote on tortured imaginings
that pin the body to a bed: eight for,
and four against. Other business:
the ranking of lesser demons and
their merits, whose ears were knives,
whose bowels instruments of grief,
whose cloud of furies released
into the dark. Meeting adjourned:
on a date to be determined in a year
distant as a dream of gardens
where lovers sleep in mussel shells
or curl themselves around enormous
berries, gluttonied in sleep, blessed
with unknowingness of the burning
nest, the wretcheds of this room.

Sanderling

So often I'm mistaken
for a stint or red knot.
Tonight, alone for once,
I am entirely myself,
piercing the ground that soon
will be submerged again.
I need feeding, my body
gray-speckled like clouds
when a storm is coming on.
Yes, I am small. My beak
is a streak of lightning
breaking through the sand.

a wake of vultures / a deceit of lapwings

Rubric of an Unacceptable Year

That year was full of typos, incomplete—
its argument was difficult to track.
It was submitted late and did not meet
the standards of a passing year. The lack
of a thesis was hard to overlook.
That year contained clichés, its thinking slack,
its words unclear. The liberties it took
with truth affected how the reader read
that year. That year was rushed. That year forsook
good scholarship, made claims without a shred
of proof. Sloppy, it barely scrutinized
its sources. That year repeated what it said
five pages back. That year was not revised.
There's evidence that year was plagiarized.

Anguish

On the spelling corrector on my computer,
when I click on English, the alternative that
comes up is Anguish. Like the suburbs, the
campus can be the site of pastoral, or the
fantasy of pastoral—the refuge, the ivory tower.
But also like the suburbs, it is the site of those
perennials of the literary imagination John
Updike names as "discontent, conflict, waste,
sorrow, fear."
—ELAINE SHOWALTER

In the Hall of Passing Snidery,
we made remarks called barbs
because they hooked inside of us,
lodged where even now we cannot
pull them out without more hurt.
But what comfort in our smallness,
as if to know that campus—buildings
in collapse, the wounded sculpture
of the founding father's head—
was to know the minor damage
mediocrity could do, restricted
to a few acres at the water's edge.
No one would ever hear of us.
Our talent was plotting how best
to kill ambition, with a memo
or an ad-hoc committee convened
in the dank of June. We taught
grammar and logic in the Atrium
of Ache, rhetoric of cut-to-the-quick,
arithmetic of whom to subtract first.
We taught the honed angles
of geometry and music in sharps.

We taught astronomy,
the magnificent gravity of regret.
As for our young colleagues—
in the Unfitness Center, we tied stones
to their waists to make them sink.
In the Great Hall of Belittling,
in the Cafeteria of Our Hungers,
in the Conference Room of No
One Gets Out of This Alive,
we observed their defeated slump.
We have made you like us, we said.
To those we despised the most,
we gave tenure, a permanent office
in the Department of Hate, a certificate
stuck with the seal of our discipline,
each name calligraphied in red,
as if there really were a soul
to sign away, and all of us overseen
by some administrative devil
in the Center of Faustian Bargaining.

Early Mornings in Anger and Thaw

During the worst weeks, I walked.
It was a matter of circling
the neighborhood I knew so well,
no looking was needed, down the hill,
then right at Rolling Road to the long
curve that took me near campus.
Sometimes I entered, hoping to meet no one.
I took the lane that led by dumpsters
where students had puked the night before,
violent breakage of beer bottles,
crushed red cups in the dirt.
In those weeks, I barely stopped walking,
stopped worrying about the ones
who were trying to hurt me—
colleagues, I used to call them.
I walked where grass became muck,
litter of cigarette butts,
a torn textbook in the bushes.
I felt most comfortable there, walking
the indecent landscape of the young,
where wanting was not yet
something to be thrown away.
I walked to the edge of a field
where goalposts sloped in the wind,
and the netting lashed itself, little thwack
of knots, almost as if in punishment.
Then right and right again, walking
with the traffic, the rumbling
uncertainty of what was coming next.
How we hear what hurts us often
before we see it—most collisions
approach too quickly to avoid.
I walked alongside the street,

kicking dust and the dust of glass,
then stood at the crossing
where cars were as likely to run the light
as to slam the brakes.
I was tired, and in another time
I would have taken the quick way home.
Instead I kept walking toward
the fenced areas where strangers lived.
And soon there were longer pauses
between houses, long grasses,
and the same castigating wind
like a slap across the face. And there,
except for a listing shack on a hill,
I was alone, a little hunched myself.
Now I walked until Morgnec
changed to River and then turned back.
A few minutes from town, at the turnoff
to the auto shop, I thought about rumors,
the junkyard scraps of meaning
made by words, what we learn when others
show us ourselves in a cracked mirror.
During the worst weeks, I was always
walking through slush and fracture.
I walked to the corner of Cedar
where my house was squat in the mud,
and somewhere beneath the cold,
I had to believe little cups of gold,
the sharp, green stems of crocuses
were poking through, I had to believe,
perennial and resistant,
refusing to be halted by the snow.

Northern Cardinal

I punctuate the branch,
a color known as anger,
the sharp scribble of my head.
Another name for snow
is erasure of the ground.
I speak to it, reminding winter
of complaints I've sent,
my reports into the air.
Who hasn't heard me speak
if not the birds and other birds.
I've seen them chattering
behind their wings,
how they open their beaks
to take the cursive worm.
I am sitting in my own
brightness, a red correction
drawn across the page.

Wild Kingdom

You have seen the oldest lion taken down,
first by the one hyena with the glinting smile,
and the blood then calling to the rest, the cackle
circling in the dust and shine of the day,
jabbing with their snouts at the golden hide,
its line of scars like faded markings in a book.
And the teeth now grip at flesh, a new cut
incised in the long history of this creature
who begins to turn and turn, searching for escape.
But didn't, you ask, the lion crouch
in the whispering grass for many years?
Wasn't the antelope, its legs like slender pencils,
snapped by the tremendous power of that jaw?
Perhaps all creatures end this way, muscle split to bone
and hunger fed on what was once magnificent.
Perhaps this is merely entertaining.
You watch the lion's eyes, shifting from amber
to something you call fear. One day,
you'll be the old lion. This is the grand narrative.
And the hyenas are always coming for a kill.
Already you can see the hunched shape of their spines,
up ahead the lurching movements. You hear
voices, almost familiar in their laughter.

Advanced Poetry

Sometimes we met with our questions
in the small furrows of a page,
such as the matter of a swan asleep
beneath a tree or the rain that drags
green apples from the branch.
I liked them most at their arrival,
when the classroom was a temporary field,
open and wide-skyed in all directions.
But it was possible to fear them too,
their faces difficult to read as any text
and the chalk dust like a shadow.
The weather could turn. The light
could go and leave behind a ground
they would not dig into—that kind
of work, they said, was violence.
And I was rarely human to their eyes,
more like a sharp pebble plucked
from a shoe. To me they were
so often a long stretch of wildflowers,
as if a uniformity of purple
blossoms planted near the highway,
all of them swaying together in the wind.

An Essay on Cruelty

All day I watch her speaking
on the hill, the former ambassador
who knows the political is snow,
which gives beneath her feet. She says,
I don't know how to put this into words.
It's hard explaining cruelty—only
some have felt the coldness of its cut.
It must be frozen where she sits.
Once I saw a film about the Bolshoi.
Before the ballet director lost half
his sight, attacked with acid on the street,
his right eye a blizzard of unseeing,
there were months of warnings,
small shivers in the night.
Sometimes I used to tremble
with the weather, waiting for news
of when the wind would blow.
The president writes wherever
the ambassador went the world
turned bad. And her face on the screen
is a field of deepening furrows.
Once I saw myself in anyone
who stood at the center of a storm.
Cruelty has a pattern possible to trace—
it's not all swirl and bluster, but brief
intensities of nothing going wrong.
I'm watching late into the dark.
Someone speaks about *the chilling effect,*
that threats are like December,
the way the season turns the surface
of a lake unbreakable, while
underneath a body batters against
the water gone suddenly to glass.

Field Notes on the Disruption of Flight Patterns

it may take minutes for the noise to reach us
        the leader's screech the long cacophony of response

they're writing letters in the air we like to say
        but as we watch a wedge of birds may separate

ignore the quill's propelling point
        the one out front may hesitate too weak or only tasting hunger

we want to find a story in the faltering
        the way a multitude can follow days or weeks

and then will swerve the V dispersed the sky
        become illiterate the bodies nothing more than lost

Honor Board Hearing

The student says, he carried everywhere his loaded hurts, each pain a hollow point, a panic made of lead. It was better not to trigger him. When he smiled, his lips moved like a small machine. He was always waiting outside my door, his presence consistent as a ticking clock. Once he told me, I want to take as much of your time as possible. And in the poem he showed me a gun, the clicking it could make, that a mouth might kiss it. How cold the room when I sat facing him. And the vigilance of hairs along my neck. I think of the way he shifted in a chair, the spring-tension of his hand—the safety off, the high velocity of my fear.

Blue-Winged Teal

I watch the figures bend
to throw torn bread into the harbor.
They turn away from signs
nailed at the water's threshold,
the warnings faded on a piece of wood.
Do not, don't feed the birds.
Their gift, shredded like paper,
floats across the surface
of the world.
                Oh, civil predators.
They think to hold
their teeth around my neck.
This late spring, I lift into the open.
I throw myself into the biting
air that pulls against my wings.

Honor Board Hearing

The student says, the loneliness of objects bothers me. My roommate leaves a ballpoint pen abandoned on her desk. Or someone forgets a backpack on a bench. I am compelled by its sad slump, the mouth of its zipper opening into dark. A shirt. A laptop. A key to a door I've never seen. I would give each relinquished thing the welcome of my hands. Once I was surrendered in this way, misplaced like a cell phone in a midnight theater. Now I do the finding. I save an earring from neglect, pin it to my own lobe. I rescue books, their inky grief of marginalia.

Incompetence or Malice

Watching the pundits argue
        the motive of the president—
if the man in the columned house doesn't grasp
        the weight of power,

how it's like a figure made of bronze
        one could knock from a mantle,
or if he understands and uses it quite precisely
        as a cudgel to the skull—

watching them speak, I'm reminded of my own
        small contact with power's metal gleam,
those people who for a year
        debated what to do with me,

was I a plaque to hang
        in honor on a wall, or a name to be rubbed out,
power always larger than it seemed,
        and the ones who carried it

less ready than they believed to lift the burden,
        but how they loved power,
patinaed, bearing the fingerprints
        of those who came before,

and how they would rather bruise their hands
        than give it back,
and doesn't that sound like the man
        whose every entrance is marked

by a marching band,
       and by the side of a white glove angled in salute,
so what if I waited in conference rooms,
       waiting to be retrieved

from the dim spaces of my uncertainty,
       and sitting across from them, all of us still
as visitors to a gallery
       where the art requires reverence,

I couldn't tell was this incompetence or malice,
       no one speaking, power
cold between us, beautiful
       as the burnished torso of a god.

Field Notes on Departure

when you are leaving what hates you
        prepare to be further despised for choosing

to leave like the bird that abandons its flock
        pecked and prodded on the crowded wire

pushed about but flying away its tail feather
        plucked how dare you leave us how dare you

the bird small burning at the soft of its neck
        when you are leaving the place where ambition

is earthbound limbs sunk in the mud and the stars
        how ungleaming you leave us how dare you

and when you are leaving consider the tree
        you have seen full of leaves until like a shake

of a paintbrush the sky is spattered with ink
        the flock taking off a bird left perching

in the cold of its loneliness and the sound O
        the screeching how dare you how dare you

Sun Salutations with Betrayal and Departure

Although this room is full of moving,
sweating people—all of us lunging forward,
or folding ourselves in tangled shapes,
obedient to Sanksrit names we're told
mean mountain, plank, dog—
downward facing, I feel a sudden anger.
After, I talk with a woman.
For years I've called her a friend.
We lean damp against the mirror.
If there were a Sanskrit name for what I am
to her, it would be *following flower,*
the loyalty of a blossom that opens
beside its colleague on the branch.
We talk of our work. And I sense, the way
spines know the limits of their curvature,
that she has lied to me. I feel the places
where the teacher touched my face with oil,
while I lay on the mat like a sleeper, insensate.
Months from now, my friend will explain
the truth is a limb that can bend,
words too a flexibility, contortion
learned through daily practice.
What else should I say?—soon others
will try to break me like a small bone in the foot.
Soon she will not place a hand
on the hunched sadness of my shoulder.
I will be left to learn the correct pose
of warrior for myself, heels aligned,
belly tightened as if waiting for a punch.
If there were a Sanskrit name
for what she will do by doing nothing
to help me, it would be *passive river.*
It would be *silent moon of cowardice.*

It would be *kneeling hyena with averted gaze.*
Or, put unbeautifully, she could have warned
that others were trying to hurt me.
And there are injuries no stretching can undo—
we live with the twinge in the back.
Months from now, I won't say goodbye,
my leaving not marked by a mallet
dragged on the edge of a singing bowl,
harmonics emerging from the empty
slope of the vessel. The divine
in me won't bow to the divine in her.
There will be no pressing together of palms.

a flight of swallows / an exaltation of larks

Exit Report

In this report, the poet will retrieve
     her heart from the gods—
  you'll know her heart by the way
it was feasted on. In this report,
     she'll unchain her wrists from the rock.
  When the ocean arrives,
she'll already be gone. In this report,
     she'll guide her ship unruined
  through a strait of teeth and swirling.
Reporting, she won't be a monster
     at the heart of a maze. Or will
  be monstrous and follow the thread,
rescue her bull-headed body
     from the punishment of kings.
  In this report, she won't be held
in the downy smothering of a swan. Nothing
     will trick her with desire's shifting shape.
  What she reports will make everything
gold—the table where she sat
     so many years, the years themselves
  now hardened in their cruelty.
Such glimmering in this report.
     Nor will she be turned
  to stone when facing herself
in the polished shield of this report.
     The snakes of her won't stop their hissing.
  In this report, the wax won't melt,
her wings incapable of not beating.
     Look, how she loves the heat,
  the feather-singe, and the water
far below, like a darkness she is leaving.

Honor Board Hearing

We were fighting in the courtyard, says the student, faces blinking down on us. That's the problem with this place—someone is always staring from a window, and everywhere is glass. Always a clear line between me and the rest. This must be what an animal feels at the zoo, viewed but not seen, those watchers sympathetic to the captivity of the beast, how human the creature seems, the way it forms its majestic hand into a fist.

Mallard

Can you understand
that I tried to hide?
You've seen the green
iridescence of my head,
that I was a cobalt streak
in flight. I could never
be a mist, the ash
feathers of modesty.
I didn't ask to gleam,
to glide in my gemstone
glittering across the water,
bank faded into shadow
and the trees going plain.
Only in summer, molted
of myself, might I be
safe in my unshimmering,
a body standing drab
in the narrow grass.

Fairy Tale with Laryngitis and Resignation Letter

You remember the mermaid makes a deal,
her tongue evicted from her throat,
and moving is a knife-cut with every step.
This is what escape from water means.
Dear Colleagues, you write, for weeks
I've been typing this letter in the bright
kingdom of my imagination. Your body
is a ship of pain. Pleasure is when you climb
the rocks and watch the moonlight
touching everywhere you want to go,
a silver world called faraway. Dear Colleagues,
you write, this place is a few sentences
contained by the cursor's rippling barrier—
what happened here is only beaks
and brackets, the serif's liquid stroke.
The old story has witches, a prince in love
with the surging silence of women,
a knife that turns the water red. You write,
Dear Colleagues, now these years are filed
in the infinite oceans of bureaucracy.
Everything bleaches or fades. In other words,
goodbye. Sometimes it's possible to walk,
although you've been told inside the oyster
shell of your heart, there is no soul.
Creatures like you must end as a spray of salt,
green droplets floating breathless in the air.

Postcard to the Colonial Town Where I Lived for Eight Years

You've lost your red-brick charm and smell of mold.
Each night I hear a skittering, a mouse
inside the walls of you. Whatever hold
on me has crumbled like your customhouse,
your columns propped with planks, the Chesapeake
lapping your foundation. Old is not the same
as prized, and you are old, my dear. You leak
when there is rain. There's rotting in your frame.
I've learned from you affections need white gloves,
a preservationist. Without thick glass,
without humidity control, our loves
are papers yellowing. Forget rubbed brass.
I'm done with monuments, historic signs.
Your streets go nowhere—crooked lines.

Memory of a Year with Allusions to the Greeks

When I had company, it might have been
                            the classicist who sat with me—
he would have called that year *cloud-cuckoo-land.*

                 We worked in a place of claw and pinion. Beak.
Outside, a shadowbird was cawing
            on the branch, all signs gesturing at catastrophe.

Some ancient playwright said
                grief's an avalanche whose weight we cannot stop,
of course, I'm paraphrasing here.

                  We rolled boulders to a hilltop.
We commiserated in the maze of our small suffering.
        The Greeks would have named the classicist *kind natured.*

He told me once he hated
               how that year had smashed the clay of him,
breathed anger in his lungs.

          Beyond my window, the great green lawn remained
indifferent, and in the warmer months,
        students drowsed on towels, golden figures in the light.

And then, sudden as a crane that lowers gods onto the stage,
      the classicist and I were both leaving, a strange departure
from the mythology. We were leaving

        even the monster of that year—the many-headed one
so hungry it would feed upon its own serrated self.
                I don't remember our goodbye.

I hope somewhere he's still explaining
        what the Greeks believed about pain, how the body keeps on
bleeding and we spit the poison out.

                        That snake-bitten year—I'll strike it
in revenge for how it wounded us. I'll string the bow.
                I'll send the arrow through a dozen iron rings.

Swarm

Years after I left, the bees began
to build in the places I used to fill
with the syrup of my anger—
ten thousand bees performing
their gold hexagonal work
in the highest rooms, until the heat
of that autumn pushed them out.
They died on the stairs. They battered
against the glistening narrative
of a stained-glass window.
From the floor below, one could hear
the uncanny beating of bodies,
how like a sullen murmuring
those wings. Honey dripped
from the walls like a dream of plenty.
When even the stinger is protected,
how to rid oneself of such buzzing?
Search for holes. Seal the entry-points.
Choke the corners with smoke.
And still the bees wouldn't go.
Something admirable in staying—
reflective facets of their eyes,
furred tongue to suck the nectar,
these droning specks, these moving
clouds of fury closing in.

Osprey

From the height of my platform
there was a river. I know
that thing you built for me
was intended as display.
Ahead, silvered surfaces reflecting,
then dark, the long mirror
dimming each day.
There was power in reaching
my wingspan to its glossy length.
I might let you see the rapt
mask of my profile, my eyes
like stones lifted from the dirt.
You who make a nest for weakness,
what could you know of me.
Something of ground and sky.
What could you do but cut a frame
and peg it in the swampy land,
as if a wooden stand
could look to me like home.

Ira Furor Brevis Est

—HORACE, *Epistles*

If the anger isn't madness anymore,
you find it by dredging the mud
at the bottom of yourself, clear cove
gone cloudy. And soon you are driving
that town again, those streets
called Cannon and College, the mire
of waterfront swirling in your view,
those buildings where rage circled
like badly vented air. And here,
in this poem, you wander conference rooms
and find the secret files of your offenses—
that time you swept tradition
in the trash like a broken porcelain cup,
and how they couldn't forgive you
for holding the broom, because goddamn
that place, its antique custom of hating
whatever it thought did not belong,
and how you didn't, and now the anger
begins to fill in scenes you once forgot.
His face the red of drinking whiskey
in his office. Her eyes a dull chalkboard
or a window fogged with weather.
And the poem returns you to summer's wet,
the haze of August touching
the coolness of your current mind.
And you see how easily you left behind
the charming artifacts of that place,
chimneys smoky black with their own
grievances, landscape of blue
herons quill-sharp among the reeds.

Pardon

When the president signs a pardon,
I try imagining if I could grant
forgiveness on thick paper—
could I offer the guilty something
like a word erased, only a smudge-mark
left as evidence. This week murderers
were given the clean of clemency.
Long before that, it was the sheriff
known for his prison of tents so hot
in the summer shoes melted to the floor.
Imagine a world of Wite-Out,
correction fluid covering all crimes
with the thick obscurity of paint.
Imagine delete-delete. I make a list
of anyone who might petition me.
As for the president, he's filing away
his rogues for mercy at a later date,
although to accept a pardon means
admitting one *did the thing,* lied to the FBI
or tampered with the ink-black truth.
In the small democracy of the self,
I'm considering my own power to absolve.
I'm writing my name in the style
of a head of state. I'm trying to imagine
if a pardoner can ever scratch out,
as if with thick marker, the fraud
and larceny committed by the past.

Field Notes on the Hatchling

not helpless when she's born
              all pink-eraser skin and open-

beak not throat of orange hunger
              swallowing the sky not eyes

sealed shut like tender envelopes
      but feathers fully formed and wide-

awake but breaking from the egg
      but voice that shrieks much sharper

than its paper-weight but plume
      a downy instinct ending in a barb

Small Miseries or Large

Some fights, we say, are sized to fit neatly
as papers on a lectern, perhaps a lesson
about the failing task of speech, language
like leaves now scattering the field.
Some fights demand a national audience,
both video and sound, the lapel microphone
with its sidelong, hidden line. Tonight,
the chyron on the news is whooshing past
our sight, WHITE HOUSE RESORTS TO LIES,
the windswept avenue of politics so like
the bookish pathways we have walked.
Regard the antique buildings of the state,
bicameral and domed. And, look,
a boathouse gifted by the graduates,
class of 1921. It's all a matter of proportion—
so much depends on ceiling heights,
the echoing halls. Some fights fit anywhere
there's room to seat a full committee.
These structures hold small miseries or large.
WHITE HOUSE REPEATS FALSE CLAIM, the TV says.
And in the classroom, there's a stub of chalk,
a blackboard smudged and indecipherable,
where hands have rubbed away the words.

Honor Board Hearing

The student says, all words belong to all of us, the way a keg is shared among a thousand plastic cups. Some nights I drink the sentences my girlfriend speaks. I stand on couches. I spin the room. I throw my voice across a parking lot. The source I cite is slurred or tilting on the path, the sky a darkened sheet of paper. What is generosity if not this giving, all words passed hand to hand, these paragraphs that float around us in the air like smoke, good tokes of language we take into our lungs and then exhale.

Course Evaluation

In that room, we held a tiny bird,
unfolding its corners first,
returning it to flattened paper,
touching the creases left behind.
We made and unmade cranes,
the wings uneven, beaks too big.
We grew tired of repetition.
How often we crumpled a tail
in crimping it or crushed a neck
with longing to form a floating thing.
We learned this work requires
sharp points, an understanding
of the edge. Eventually, we learned
the fierce precision of our hands.

Song for a Grackle in the
Kroger Parking Lot

Don't hate the scavenger.
In daylight, it's purple-
stained, iridescence

of oil spilled on asphalt,
its body like a rag rung out.
Love, instead, that groups

are known as plagues,
aggrievances. Love
the reflective eye that stares,

how everywhere is home.
Time has a way of driving
over us. Love the choice

the grackle makes—
to tear the silver insides
of a candy wrapper,

to pick apart the leavings,
to sing and sing despite
the rusted metal of its throat.

AUTHOR'S NOTES

Poems in this book were written in conversation with pieces by John Ashbery, Paul Celan, Louise Glück, and Larry Levis.

Academic mobbing is defined as "a form of bullying in which members of a department gang up to isolate or humiliate a colleague" (*Chronicle of Higher Education*, June 2009). Sociologist Kenneth Westhues has created a checklist of sixteen indicators of mobbing, which include a "shared conviction that the target needs some kind of formal punishment," "emotion-laden, defamatory rhetoric about the target in oral and written communications," and "the adding up of the target's real or imagined venial sins to make a mortal sin that cries for action."

Elaine Showalter's *Faculty Towers: The Academic Novel and Its Discontents* offers an engaging overview of the literary genre known as the "campus novel."

The "Honor Board" poems are works of imagination and do not pertain to specific real cases.

CPSIA information can be obtained
at www.ICGtesting.com
Printed in the USA
LVHW091422270221
680109LV00031B/712

9 780807 174128